MW01611114

How Can I
WIN
Over
Worry?

Charles R. Swindoll

INSIGHT FOR LIVING

HOW CAN I WIN OVER WORRY?

By Charles R. Swindoll

Charles R. Swindoll has devoted his life to the clear, practical teaching and application of God's Word and His grace. Chuck currently is the senior pastor of Stonebriar Community Church in Frisco, Texas, but his listening audience extends far beyond this local church body. As a leading program in Christian broadcasting, *Insight for Living* airs in major Christian radio markets around the world, reaching people groups in languages they can understand. Chuck's extensive writing ministry has also served the body of Christ worldwide, and his leadership as president and now chancellor of Dallas Theological Seminary has helped prepare and equip a new generation for ministry.

Published By:
IFL Publishing House
A Division of Insight for Living
Post Office Box 251007
Plano, Texas 75025-1007

The text of this booklet was adapted by Michael J. Svigel, Th.M., Ph.D., Dallas Theological Seminary from the original outlines and transcript of Charles R. Swindoll's sermon, "How Can I Win Over Worry?" Copyright © 1984 by Charles R. Swindoll, Inc. This message appears in the series, *Questions Christians Ask*.

Editor in Chief: Cynthia Swindoll, President, Insight for Living
Executive Vice President: Wayne Stiles, Th.M., D.Min.,
        Dallas Theological Seminary
Theological Editor: Brianna Barrier Engeler, M.A., Biblical Studies,
        Dallas Theological Seminary
Copy Editors: Jim Craft, M.A., English, Mississippi College
        Melanie Munnell, M.A., Humanities,
        The University of Texas at Dallas
Project Coordinator, Creative Ministries: Kim Gibbs,
        Trinity Valley Community College, 1991–1993
Project Coordinator, Communications: Karen Berard, B.A.,
        Mass Communications, Texas State University-San Marcos
Proofreader: Paula McCoy, B.A., English, Texas A&M University-Commerce
Cover Designer: Kari Pratt, B.A., Commercial Art,
        Southwestern Oklahoma State University
Production Artist: Nancy Gustine, B.F.A., Advertising Art,
        University of North Texas
Cover Image: © 2009 Insight for Living
Photo Source: Jupiterimages Corporation

ISBN: 978-1-57972-831-1
Printed in the United States of America

How Can I
WIN
Over
Worry?

A Letter from Chuck

No one will ever know how much energy has been consumed by the human race through worry.

We are the most anxious among all of God's creatures. Our phobias number in the hundreds. Our diseases spring from stress more often than any other source. Our battles with common problems such as insomnia, obesity, addictions, and headaches frequently trace their roots to deep-seated unrest in our souls. And our struggles with pessimism, lack of humor, frustration, and old-fashioned grumpiness often stem from anxiety.

What nervous, tense creatures we are!

Surely God did not design our bodies to endure such self-imposed stress. Nor does this intensity represent the way His children are to model His message of peace.

I wish I could say I was beyond the effects of worry, that I've fought and conquered that battle and moved on to other spiritual conflicts. But the truth is, we're in this fight together. You and me. Nobody is immune to the disease of anxiety; nobody has been inoculated against the infection of stress; nobody is insulated against the high pressures of a fallen world.

But there's good news! We *can* have victory over worry. In this booklet, we'll arm ourselves with spiritual weapons against worry—divine alternatives to anxiety. And when we put these biblical principles into practice, they will bring refreshing peace instead of panic . . . rest instead of rush . . . tranquility instead of turmoil.

In God's incomprehensible peace,

Chuck Swindoll

Charles R. Swindoll

How Can I WIN Over *Worry?*

I would like to dedicate this booklet about worry to Martha—in fact, to all the "Marthas" out there. Understand that a "Martha" can be a man or a woman . . . married or single . . . young, middle-aged, or older . . . a new Christian or a person who has walked with the Lord for many, many years. A "Martha" might be a person who is worth an enormous amount of money or a person who can barely get along financially. One simple word defines a "Martha": *worry.*

We all know about worry:

- It's interest paid on trouble before it comes due.

- It's a circle of inefficient thoughts whirling about a pivot of fear.

- It's the only game in which, even when you guess right, you still don't feel any better.

To help understand what characterizes a "Martha," let's look at Luke 10:38–42.

> Now as they were traveling along, [Jesus] entered a village; and a woman named Martha welcomed Him into her home. She had a sister called Mary, who was seated at the Lord's feet, listening to His word. But Martha was distracted with all her preparations; and she came up to Him and said, "Lord, do You not care that my sister has left me to do all the serving alone? Then tell her to help me." But the Lord answered and said to her, "Martha, Martha, you are worried and bothered about so many things; but only one thing is necessary, for Mary has chosen the good part, which shall not be taken away from her."

When I read those words, I can't help but smile with understanding. Whoever judges Martha is a bit of a hypocrite, in my opinion, because we *all* have a bit of Martha in us. Here was a responsible, conscientious, determined woman who had a deadline to meet. She was preparing a meal for the Savior, which probably did not happen that often during His busy ministry years. On top of that, she had a sister who wouldn't get up and help! And if that weren't bad enough, Jesus peered into her soul and diagnosed her as a worrier.

Jesus was saying, in effect, "Martha, your self-imposed assignments are more than you and a dozen like you are able to meet. Really only one thing is needed, and you're missing it. Spend time with Me." A friend of mine once suggested that Jesus's comment might mean, "Only a sandwich will do. Just one dish. You don't need to match all the china and put out your best crystal and choose your finest linens and make this some big headache. All you need to do is pour a bowl of soup." Jesus asked Martha to let go of all her worries and to focus on Him.

At this point it might help to understand the origin of our English word *worry*. It comes from the old high German word *wurgen*, meaning "to strangle."[1] It originally brought to mind the image of a mental or emotional choking or strangling. Have you ever experienced that feeling of mental strangulation? It can be really frightening. We panic. Our minds race from place to place, from resource to resource. We're seized with the uncertainty of being able to handle our situation. And we're confident that things will get worse, not better. In a state of mental strangulation, we can't begin to think clearly. More often than not, the problem that has seized us is quite small, but we've made it big.

The Faces Worry Wears

Mentally strangled and seized with fear, Martha began to wear several faces, the familiar faces of worry that we have all worn from time to time. Look at them with me.

The first face of worry is *angry and impatient*. Read Luke 10:40.

> But Martha was distracted with all her preparations; and she came up to Him and said, "Lord, do You not care that my sister has left me to do all the serving alone? Then tell her to help me."

Martha was irritated that her sister wouldn't get with it. She was even irritated at Jesus for not realizing that she had needs in the kitchen and for His not ordering Mary to come and help.

The second face of worry is *rushed and hurried*. Martha was "distracted with all her preparations" (Luke 10:40), and Jesus said,

"Martha, Martha, you are worried and bothered about so many things" (10:41). Preoccupied with our anxiety, we drive much too fast. We don't move through life, we ricochet. We bounce from one wall to another, from one corner to another in our hurry-worry syndrome.

The third face of worry is *fearful and panicked*. What a number that does on us! Some of us become so consumed by fear that we can no longer live normal lives or have normal relationships. I once read of a woman named Marjorie Goff who stayed in her house from the time she was 31 until the age of 61 because she was afraid to go outside.[2] Horrible mental strangulation. When worry overcomes us, we sometimes become so afraid and panic-stricken that we don't even act like ourselves and we don't respond to stressful situations in a sensible manner.

A fourth face of worry is *pessimistic and critical*. Frustrated over her situation, Martha lashed out. She became harshly critical of her sister. And she even dared to demand that Jesus fix the problem her way.

Those are the familiar faces of worry: angry and impatient . . . rushed and hurried . . . fearful and panicked . . . pessimistic and critical.

Ever find yourself wearing one of those faces? They can cause all kinds of damage. Spiritually, *worry assaults our faith*. That fog of unbelief blots out God. We see only horizontally, think only earthly, and fail to appreciate a heavenly perspective. Physically, *worry steals our health*. How many physicians do you know who will tell you (and I know of many) that more than half their patients are ill because of stress? Just *stress*. Worry has driven their bodies to "strangle" themselves. Emotionally, *worry destroys our peace*. The tranquility necessary for us to function with any measure of maturity and calm resolve is gone. We can't sleep; we can't eat; we can't digest; we can't rest; we can't even enjoy leisure.

We are worried, worried, worried.

Divine Alternatives to Worry

So far, we've only considered the human side of worry. We've studied the faces worry wears and the damage worry does. Now I want to look at what God says about worry. He has an infinite number of solutions to offer, and He picks and chooses the things that will work best for our individual needs. Then He says to us, in effect, "Now do that. Even though you don't get human counsel from anyone else, do that. It will work. It will help."

My fear is that you'll read this as just another "how to" guide on worry and then go right back about your anxious business, hurrying and worrying over your meals and your future and your lifestyle. If you promise not to do that, I'll invite you to travel with me to three sections of Scripture that reveal God's alternatives to worry. They aren't new, they don't rhyme, and they won't seem very profound or scientific or even very clever from a worldly mind-set. But they work. Every time I put them into practice, these three things work:

1. A willingness to wait
2. A commitment to Christ
3. A priority of prayer

Let's look at each of these in some detail.

A Willingness to Wait

Isaiah 40 talks about a *willingness to wait*. Look at the last few verses—28 through 31. These verses come on the heels of an argument. The people in the land of Israel are arguing with God, shaking their fists heavenward, screaming their doubts and their unbelief in their comfortless situation and wondering where God is and why He isn't meeting their perceived needs.

> Why do you say, O Jacob, and
>   assert, O Israel,
> "My way is hidden from the LORD,
> And the justice due me escapes the
>   notice of my God"? (Isaiah 40:27)

Those are the words of a worrier. First of all, the worrier thinks, "God's gone. So I'm going to have to take charge. He's absent, and I'm present. I can't see Him; I can't feel Him. He's obviously not working; He's hidden Himself from me." And then the worrier begins to think, "I've got my rights, and if He's not going to take care of the justice due me then I'll take care of it myself. I'll get the counsel I need to help me make it happen." And you'll always find people who'll agree with you and help you to accomplish what you want to do . . . usually with a catch or for a fee.

And then Isaiah wrote, "Do you not know? Have you not heard?" (Isaiah 40:28). Have you ever been worried and have someone say, "Don't you know what to do?" Or, "Haven't you heard about such and such?" I mean, it's the most comfortless kind of counsel you can imagine. Unless, of course, it's true. You don't know, you haven't heard, or maybe you've forgotten. Isaiah asks these penetrating questions and uses them to lead into a wonderful reminder of truth. As a matter of fact, all of Isaiah 40 is made up of great questions and answers. Start at verse 12.

> Who has measured the waters in
>   the hollow of His hand,
> And marked off the heavens by
>   the span,
> And calculated the dust of the earth
>   by the measure,
> And weighed the mountains in a
>   balance
> And the hills in a pair of scales?
> Who has directed the Spirit of
>   the Lord,
> Or as His counselor has informed
>   Him? (40:12–13)

The answer? *No one.*

> With whom did He consult and
>   who gave Him understanding?
> And who taught Him in the path of
>   justice and taught Him knowledge
> And informed Him of the way of
>   understanding? (40:14)

Response? *No one.*

> To whom then will you liken God?
> Or what likeness will you compare
> with Him? (Isaiah 40:18)

Again? *No one.*

Now to verse 21.

> Do you not know? Have you not
> heard?
> Has it not been declared to you
> from the beginning?
> Have you not understood from the
> foundations of the earth?
> It is He who sits above the circle of
> the earth,
> And its inhabitants are like grass-
> hoppers. (40:21–22)

God isn't biting His nails over humans. He isn't having a breakdown because of the situation on earth. Look at verses 25 and 26:

> "To whom then will you liken Me
> That I would be his equal?" says the
> Holy One.
> Lift up your eyes on high. (40:25–26)

God alone is the answer to all of these questions. Once again in verse 28:

> Do you not know? Have you not
>   heard?
> The Everlasting God, the Lᴏʀᴅ, the
>   Creator of the ends of the earth
> Does not become weary or tired.
> His understanding is inscrutable.
>   (40:28)

Obviously, every situation is within the scope of God's knowledge. *He is the Lord*. And that means He's over all and above all and through all and in all. He's certainly aware of our circumstances. He's almighty and all-powerful, so He certainly has the ability to handle our needs. He's the Creator of the ends of the earth. We can't hide from Him nor will He from us. And the good news is that He "does not become weary or tired. His understanding is inscrutable" (Isaiah 40:28).

Boy, that's good theology! It's like blowing the dust off of a Theology 101 book and coming back to basics. Look up! What's God like? Well, He's the Creator of the earth. He is absolutely omnipotent. He is omnipresent. He is full of compassion and goodness. He will never do us wrong. He will never leave us in the lurch. He won't turn His back when we're in need of Him. But keep in mind that He may not move on *our* timetable. You see, He's everlasting. And He has a full panoramic view of our circumstances and sees our real needs. His plan for each one of us is perfect — though we may not fully understand it.

From the windows of an airplane, our big cities seem so small. I can see the whole scene. And the city that makes up most of my world seems so tiny. That's the way it is from God's perspective. It's as though He's telling us, "I know what I'm doing. I see the big picture, and I know your specific situation. I'm not tired. I'm not mopping my brow and sweating this out and wondering, 'What in the world are we going to do about that situation?' I'm not worried. I know completely well what's going on. I'm in charge."

Now look at what God does with that great strength of His. He dispenses it. He doesn't hoard it . . . He gives it! That's *grace*. Verse 29 says,

> He gives strength to the weary,
> And to him who lacks might He
>   increases power. (40:29)

You may say, "What I need is youth!" No.

> Youths grow weary and tired.
>   (40:30)

"What I need is to be in better shape." No.

And vigorous young men stumble
   badly. (40:30)

Physical fortitude isn't what we need. Nor do we need mental strength. We need to admit our weakness, to stop fighting. In fact, are you ready for the most profound counsel of Isaiah 40? Look at verse 31:

Yet those who wait for the Lord
Will gain new strength. (40:31)

Now you may be thinking, *Chuck, I was all ready for something profound and you tell me to wait*. But *that's* the profound counsel. And it's the hardest thing to do. When we worry, we refuse to wait. We traffic every available rabbit trail. We go all the way to the dead end, keep butting up against a wall, turn around bloody, and run back against another dead end . . . all because we refuse to wait.

Focus on the word *wait*. It's translated from an interesting Hebrew term. It's from a verb in the causative stem, which means that waiting will cause something to happen. Now the action of waiting is a beautiful image in Hebrew thought. The term pictures one little strand of hair that is wrapped around several other strands, which in turn are wrapped around other strands until finally a massive rope is formed.[3] And the single strand, by being wrapped around the rope, becomes as strong as the rope itself. Those who wait on the Lord will exchange their weakness for God's strength. That's the idea. In effect, those who wait take their one single strand of weakness and they weave it around the heavy, rope-like power of God. Then they become strong through their relationship with Him.

And when we wait, what will happen?

> They will mount up with wings like
>   eagles,
> They will run and not get tired,
> They will walk and not become
>   weary. (Isaiah 40:31)

We won't be exhausted at the end of the day. We will not have spent all our energy trying to work ourselves out of something. I understand that there are some situations in which we dare not wait. We don't turn into oncoming traffic on the freeway and wait for God to move the cars away. That's not the idea. But more often than not, waiting is appropriate . . . and waiting is overdue. Some of us just think we've waited long enough. But the reality is, we've just begun to wait. We've just begun to trade our weaknesses for His strength.

Going back to Isaiah 40:31, I think the reason it says we'll fly and then run and then walk—rather than the other way around—is because we first have to cultivate the right perspective. When we wait, we'll begin to grasp God's perspective on the whole situation. And His view puts us at ease.

I'm reminded of a famous *Peanuts* cartoon. Lucy and Linus are staring out a window and rain is pouring down. Lucy speaks: "Boy, look at it rain . . . what if it floods the whole world?"

Linus answers: "It will never do that. In the ninth chapter of Genesis, God promised Noah that would never happen again, and the sign of the promise is the rainbow."

Lucy responds, "You've taken a great load off my mind."

Linus answers, "Sound theology has a way of doing that." [4]

It's true! Sound theology will take a load off of our minds. But too often we follow human wisdom, not sound theology. We look all the way around us, 360 degrees, to find somebody that will understand. And all the while God waits to give us strength if we'll only look to Him. Just put the brakes on, be calm, and focus on Him. He promises to give us strength.

A Commitment to Christ

A willingness to wait must be followed by a commitment. Look at Matthew chapter 6 — the Sermon on the Mount. These two passages — Isaiah 40 and Matthew 6 — tie together because they both imply that we naturally tend to rely upon something as we deal with life. In Isaiah 40, we're confronted about relying on our own strength. And in Matthew 6, we're convicted about our tendencies to rely on our own resources. The key to this passage is found in Jesus's wise words:

> "No one can serve two masters; for either he will hate the one and love the other, or he will be devoted to one and despise the other. You cannot [not *dare* not, or *should* not, but *cannot*] serve God and wealth." (Matthew 6:24)

"Wealth" refers to our material possessions. Bucks. Stuff that has a price tag. Things we can purchase. We cannot serve God and material possessions. This doesn't mean we can't own material possessions. It doesn't mean we can't earn a living or even earn a good living. It says we can't be a *slave* of both.

I think this verse especially speaks to some of you who are enslaved to money. I don't know who you are, but I'm sure you're out there. Your preoccupation — from the early morning hours of Monday to the late evening hours of Sunday — is money and how to make more of it. How to invest it better, how to use it for your benefit later, and on and on and on. Your mind swarms with thoughts of money. You're serving it. But you can't serve God with a mind like that. Money is supposed to be a servant, not a master. It's to be used. But it will abuse you if you bow to it as your master.

So, after calling us to commit ourselves to Him, Jesus then shared a series of commands about worry. I count five of them. The word *worry* appears in Matthew 6:25, 27, 28, 31, and 34. Each time He used the same term that we read in Luke 10:41 — "Martha, Martha, you are *worried* and bothered about so many things" (emphasis added). Worry distracts us from our commitment to God, stealing our focus and placing it on earthly things.

Jesus then talked about the things we get anxious about, starting with Matthew 6:25. *We worry about the essentials of life.*

> "For this reason I say to you [see how it flows from verse 24?], do not be worried about your life, as to what you will eat or what you will drink; nor for your body, as to what you will put on. Is not life more than food, and the body more than clothing?" (6:25)

We would all answer, "Yes, it is." But to prove it, Jesus told us to do something that few of us ever do. He asked us to take a look at the birds.

> "Look at the birds of the air, that they do not sow, nor reap nor gather into barns, and yet your heavenly Father feeds them. Are you not worth much more than they?" (6:26)

When was the last time you studied the birds? For some of you, it's been months. The only birds you notice are those crows that stagger around the street and then just kind of launch themselves back up in the air. Christ's command reminds me of our old house in California where we had a patio outside our bedroom window on the second floor. A reflective coating on the big picture window kept the heat of the sun from coming in and made it difficult to see in from the outside. So it was a perfect place to watch the birds. When they came and landed on the patio, they thought they were all alone. They chirped and fiddled around and cuddled up next to each other. And they perched right on the window, right in front. I scooted right down there and just watched those little birds. They didn't seem worried; they didn't seem bothered about what was for supper.

Jesus said, "Look at the birds of the air." What a super illustration! They don't sow, they don't reap, they don't gather, they don't save, and they don't *worry*! They just fiddle around on patio roofs. They sail in, chirp, sing, and make life beautiful. And they leave us a beautiful picture of a life free from worry.

Now look at 6:27. *We worry about things we can't change.*

> "And who of you by being worried
> can add a single hour to his life?"

In other words, some things are out of our control. Like how long we will live. How tall we're going to be. What will happen to us tomorrow.

We can't change these things, but we'll worry about them. Isn't that amazing?

Verses 28 through 30 tell us that *we worry about clothing.* I'm not going to harass you about this, but Jesus gave us a helpful illustration. Let me paraphrase it for you: "You want to know about clothing? Let Me show you how I clothe My creatures. Look at the lilies. They don't work to make their own clothes." He didn't say "zinnias." And He didn't say "olive trees." Jesus said "lilies." He knew exactly what He was saying. Lilies are elegant, lovely flowers. Jesus said, in effect, "Study the lilies. Solomon in all of his glory couldn't dress himself as richly and elegantly as I've designed the lily. And yet you're going to worry so much about what you wear and what the fashion is and how you look tonight . . . or how you'll fit in with the group tomorrow."

I love what He says in verse 34:

> "Do not worry about tomorrow; for tomorrow will care for itself. Each day has enough trouble of its own." (Matthew 6:34)

Tomorrow will be bad enough. Trust me. When it's Sunday, just handle Sunday. Monday will come with its own set of cares. But it's remarkable how some of us start living Monday long before it comes. We're already into Tuesday . . . and some even have a list into Wednesday. And it's still just Sunday! Many of us aren't even ready to handle the pressures of this afternoon, but we're hassling into next week. We get way ahead of ourselves.

I did this a number of years ago when our daughter Colleen was little. She has always been so much like her daddy, and therefore she's able to relate to my world. I was busy and had big plans, so I was talking fast. I was getting ready to go somewhere, and I was a bit angry because I had overcommitted myself. So at the dinner table that night I talked fast and I ate fast. And Colleen said, "Daddy, I want to tell you what happened today. I'm going to tell you really fast."

And I said, "Okay, I understand. But why don't you talk slowly?"

She said, "I will if you'll listen slowly."

I realized that we even listen fast when we worry. We don't hear it all. We skip things like a rock on a lake, just hitting the high spots. According to Matthew 6:32, this describes a *Gentile lifestyle*. Back when Jesus was speaking, the majority of Gentiles—non-Jews—didn't know God or live according to His truth. He was saying that this is the way godless people live. God would say, in effect, "They're not My people. The heathen live like that! You say you're My people, you say I'm your Father, and you live as though you're orphaned! I care about My children. Slow down and listen to Me. I will take care of you."

And so our response should be, verse 33:

> "But seek first His kingdom and His righteousness, and all these things will be added to you." (Matthew 6:33)

Don't you wish you always lived like you believed that? Wouldn't we be easier to live with? Wouldn't we be easier to be around? Wouldn't we be better mates, better parents, better friends, better counselors? We're told, "Now here's what you need to do: commit yourself to the person of Christ, His kingdom, His righteousness, His plan."

This could be called "car talk" because we have to tell ourselves this in the morning when we get into the car. Or "mirror talk" because we have to tell ourselves this when we look at our faces first thing in the morning. No one's going to tell us this. We probably won't get this counsel from the radio. We probably won't get this counsel from a friend. This truth has to come from God. If we make a deep-seated commitment to Him and His kingdom, He promises that all the things that really matter will be provided for us.

A Priority of Prayer

In Isaiah 40, we were reminded of our tendency to rely on our own strength. God said, in effect, that we can't: "Turn it over to Me, and I'll give you strength in place of your weakness." Then in Matthew 6, we recognized our tendency to rely on ourselves and on material possessions. Jesus said, in effect, that they won't serve us: "If you do that, you can't walk with Me. *I'll* meet your needs."

As we study Philippians 4, we'll discover that we often rely on the counsel of other people. And once again, it won't work. Look at verse 4 down through verse 7. Now these words might sound like mockery if we don't keep them in proper perspective.

> Rejoice in the Lord always; again I
> will say, rejoice! (Philippians 4:4)

Believe it or not, we *can* live like that. We *can* live with a smile. We *can* live happily before God if we live worry free. Look at verse 5:

> Let your gentle spirit be known to all
> men. The Lord is near. (Philippians 4:5)

If you're walking with Him and He's a part of your day, you can add verse 6:

> Be anxious for nothing, but in every-
> thing by prayer and supplication
> with thanksgiving let your requests
> be made known to God. (4:6)

There it is. Don't worry about anything. Let God know what's on your mind. I've found that it's better in my prayer life if I don't save every-thing up for a big twenty- to thirty-minute chunk of time. Instead, I connect with Him throughout my day. When something comes that threatens to unravel me, I talk with Him. When some situation comes along that could easily make me panic, I have to immediately bring it to Him.

A friend once said to me, "I've got this thing that I'm really worrying God over these days." That's a good way to put it. Worry God over it. The wonderful thing is, though, *He can handle it.* We'll never really shock God, and He'll never tell anybody else what's worrying us. We can turn worry into an opportunity for praise and thanks-giving. And we say ahead of time, "Lord, I don't know how to handle this agenda. It looks way out of hand to me. But You've got the wisdom, and You've got the strength, and You've got the resources. I have none of those things. So I ask You to take what I can't handle."

> And the peace of God, which surpasses all comprehension, will guard your hearts and your minds in Christ Jesus. (Philippians 4:7)

Isn't that great? Peace will enter our hearts and minds in ways we can't even imagine. People will ask us, "Why aren't you worried? I mean, what's wrong with you?" Others will say, "Well, you obviously haven't really faced this situation head-on if you're responding like that!" But the truth is, we've just placed it in the Lord's hands. We don't know how it's going to work out, but we've given it to Him, so we are able to have peace.

Putting Peace into Practice

I recall one Sunday after church when I took my sons, Chuck and Curt, on a fishing trip. We had a great time. We fished with a couple of professional bass fishermen, so we learned some great pointers, learned more and more about fishing together. It was terrific. We spent the night there, got up early the next morning, fished all day, and began the drive back home. About forty miles from where we started, I was thinking about what a good time we had, and then I reached around and discovered that I didn't have my wallet!

Screech! I slammed on the brakes, whirled the pickup truck around, and zoomed in the opposite direction. The boys asked, "Where in the world are we going?"

"Well, I lost my wallet!" As I was driving down the freeway, I was thinking, *Where in the world could that thing be? Well, maybe I left it on the counter of the 7-Eleven where we stopped to get a Coke. That's the only place I can think of. Yeah, I think I did. I think I took my wallet out, opened it up, put it down there.*

We pulled up to the 7-Eleven, and I jumped out of the truck and rushed inside. "I left my wallet here. Did you happen to put it in the drawer?"

The clerk answered, "We haven't seen a wallet."

Behind me I heard Curt say, "Oh, no!"

Then the clerk said, "Why don't you look on the floor?"

I thought, *That's the dumbest thing I've ever heard.* But I looked on the floor. No wallet.

I went back out to the pickup, and I announced, "THEY DON'T HAVE IT!" Then I got the idea that we'd try to find it in the pickup. The boys and I were looking all over until I dug in that little pocket on the driver's door . . . "I FOUND THE WALLET!" I shouted. The search was over. It had been there the whole time.

As we drove back home, my boys were discussing the episode, almost as though I wasn't in the truck. "Boy, I'm glad he found it." "Oh man, do you realize how long the trip would have been if Dad hadn't found the wallet? I mean, if you've ever been around Dad when he loses anything, he's just . . ."

And then they began to get really philosophical about the whole thing. Curt said, "Dad, why do you think God let that happen?" That was a great question.

See, what Curt didn't know was that I'd been working on a lesson about worry for about three or four weeks. But I'm glad he didn't know that in light of my response to everything that had happened. So I said to them, "Curt and Chuck, God wanted me to realize just how far I've got to go in this whole thing called rest." Then we talked about giving our worries to God and finding rest in Him.

I hope you noticed that in each of the three passages we studied, a promise followed obedience. In Isaiah 40, God gives us strength in place of our weakness. Matthew 6 states that God provides for our needs when we commit to Him. And Philippians 4 states that God gives us peace when we give Him our burdens.

I have two great concerns for those of you reading this booklet about worry. First, I'm afraid that after reading the principles, you'll think, *Boy, that was a good study on worry. My wife needs to read this.* Or, *Frank should read this.* Or, *I need to give this to my brother.* I'm afraid that you'll pass this on to somebody else and fail to apply it to yourself first. Don't do that. We *all* need to take this to heart.

The second thing I'm afraid of is that you may think I'm a great model of it, that I've outgrown the need to be reminded. And somehow that lets you off the hook too. But you know what? I can impress people with great expositions on Matthew 6 and Isaiah 40 and Philippians 4 . . . until I lose my wallet. And then I become like Martha all over again. And so do you.

Everything seems to fit so well together when we're studying the Scriptures, putting the principles all together. But then our spouse walks out on us. Or the bottom drops out of our finances. Or the doctor says the X-ray isn't good or the surgery didn't turn out the way he expected.

So we all need to get serious about applying these truths. Honestly, I sometimes wonder if I'll ever get there. But I commit myself to these three things: a willingness to wait, a commitment to Christ, and a top priority of prayer. Why don't you join me right now in a prayer of commitment to winning over worry with God's peace?

> *Father, for all of those days we've lived like Martha, for all of those years we've embraced worry rather than faith, forgive us. Help us to grow up spiritually, even when we lose our wallets, when the meal isn't ready on time, when the car breaks down, or when tragedy strikes our homes. Even then may we trust and not be afraid. In Christ's name. Amen.*

We Are Here for You

If you desire to find out more about knowing God and His plan for you in the Bible, contact us. Insight for Living provides staff pastors who are available for free written correspondence or phone consultation. These seminary-trained and seasoned counselors have years of experience and are well-qualified guides for your spiritual journey.

Please feel welcome to contact your regional Pastoral Ministries by using the information below:

United States

Insight for Living
Pastoral Ministries
Post Office Box 269000
Plano, Texas 75026-9000
USA
(972) 473-5097, Monday through Friday,
8:00 a.m. – 5:00 p.m. Central time
www.insight.org/contactapastor

Australia, New Zealand, and South Pacific

Insight for Living Australia
Pastoral Care
Post Office Box 1011
Bayswater, VIC 3153
AUSTRALIA
1 300 467 444

Canada

Insight for Living Canada
Pastoral Ministries
Post Office Box 2510
Vancouver, BC V6B 3W7
CANADA
1-800-663-7639
info@insightforliving.ca

United Kingdom and Europe

Insight for Living United Kingdom
Pastoral Care
Post Office Box 348
Leatherhead
KT22 2DS
UNITED KINGDOM
0800 915 93 64
+44 (0) 1372 370 055
pastoralcare@insightforliving.org.uk

Endnotes

1. *Merriam-Webster's Collegiate Dictionary*, 11th ed. (Springfield, Mass.: Merriam-Webster, 2003), see "worry."

2. "The Fight to Conquer Fear," *Newsweek* (April 23, 1984): 66–68.

3. Francis Brown, S. R. Driver, and Charles A. Briggs, *The Brown-Driver-Briggs Hebrew and English Lexicon*, reprint ed. (Peabody, Mass.: Hendrickson, 2006), 875.

4. Charles M. Schulz, *Peanuts* cartoon, quoted in Robert L. Short, *The Parables of Peanuts* (New York: Harper & Row, 1968), 246–47. Peanuts: © United Feature Syndicate, Inc. Used by permission.

Ordering Information

If you would like to order additional booklets or request other products, please contact the office that serves you.

United States
Insight for Living
Post Office Box 269000
Plano, Texas 75026-9000
USA
1-800-772-8888
Monday through Friday,
7:00 a.m.–7:00 p.m. Central time
www.insight.org
www.insightworld.org

Australia, New Zealand, and South Pacific
Insight for Living Australia
Post Office Box 1011
Bayswater, VIC 3153
AUSTRALIA
1 300 467 444
www.insight.asn.au

Canada

Insight for Living Canada

Post Office Box 2510

Vancouver, BC V6B 3W7

CANADA

1-800-663-7639

www.insightforliving.ca

United Kingdom and Europe

Insight for Living United Kingdom

Post Office Box 348

Leatherhead

KT22 2DS

UNITED KINGDOM

0800 915 9364

www.insightforliving.org.uk

Other International Locations

International constituents may contact
the U.S. office through our Web site
(www.insightworld.org), mail queries, or
by calling +1-972-473-5136.